MIDDLE EAST LEADER

SADDAM HUSSE

Brian Wingate

The Rosen Publishing Group, Inc.,
New York

Published in 2004 by The Rosen Publishing Group, Inc.
29 East 21st Street, New York, NY 10010

First Edition

Library of Congress Cataloging-in-Publication Data

Wingate, Brian.
Saddam Hussein / by Brian Wingate.
 p. cm. — (Middle East leaders)
Includes bibliographical references and index.
Contents: Birth and childhood—Life in Baghdad—Baath takeover—
Seizing power—The Iran-Iraq War—The Gulf War—Hussein's slide—
Endgame.
ISBN 0-8239-4468-9
1. Hussein, Saddam, 1937–—Juvenile literature. 2. Presidents—Iraq—
Biography—Juvenile literature. 3. Iraq War, 2003—Juvenile literature.
[1. Hussein, Saddam, 1937– 2. Presidents—Iraq. 3. Iraq War, 2003.]
I. Title. II. Series.
DS79.66.H87W56 2003
956.7044'092—dc21

                                                    2003010575

Manufactured in the United States of America

CONTENTS

INTRODUCTION
A TYRANT'S RULES

■ Saddam Hussein's rule over Iraq caused hardship, torture, and death to millions of Muslims. He is known as the "Butcher of Baghdad" for his murderous reign.

Dust floats through the air as men push open a towering doorway. They enter a palace hall filled with riches they had only imagined before. Sparkling chandeliers hang from vaulted ceilings.

White marble staircases wind upward toward private chambers. Paintings and statues line the walls. Signs of extravagant living are everywhere. Even a toilet plunger bears a gold handle. The crowd surges forward and spreads through the palace, looting the riches. These are the common people of the Iraq. The American military forces have only days before captured Baghdad. Now its people are rejoicing and exacting a bit of retribution against their hated—and greatly feared—leader.

Iraq's vast oil resources paid for this palace. Few Iraqis, however, saw more than a fraction of the wealth that graced just one bathroom. In 2002, the average Iraqi citizen earned just $2,500 per year. President Saddam Hussein lived a life far removed from his subjects. His days were full of luxury that most can only dream of. Invading American soldiers in the spring of 2003 found $650 million in cash hidden in one of his palace walls. But Hussein's life was not easy or even enjoyable. Saddam Hussein built his empire on secrecy, power, intimidation, and terror. Most important, he built it upon his own survival. Over a period of more than twenty years, Saddam Hussein built a dictatorial regime that ruthlessly clung to power and played a high-stakes game of survival.

In the days of Hussein, citizens were scared to even look in the direction of any of his presidential palaces. Anyone approaching the grounds would be arrested. But now the palace was deserted, and the ruler was never coming home. Who is the man that inspired such fear? How did he rise to power? This is the story of the rise and fall of Saddam Hussein.

CHAPTER ONE

BIRTH AND CHILDHOOD

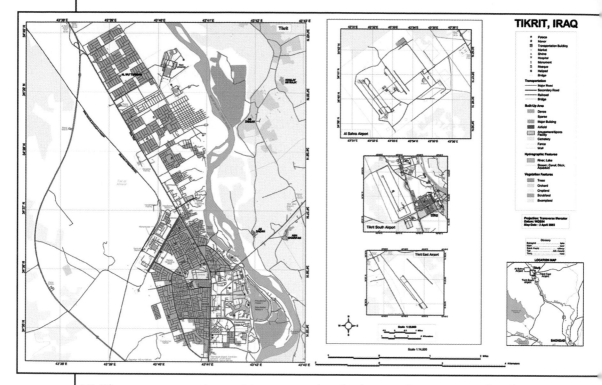

TIKRIT, IRAQ

■ These maps show Hussein's birthplace, the town of Tikrit, northwest of Baghdad. Tikrit grew wealthy under Hussein's rule. His large family living in the town also reaped the riches of his presidency.

S addam Hussein was born far from the riches that decorated the walls and grounds of his royal palaces. He was born on April 28, 1937, in the small village of al-Auja, Iraq. Al-Auja was nothing more than a gathering of mud huts on the outskirts of the town of Tikrit. Tikrit itself was a small town in northern Iraq with no electricity, running water, or paved roads. Health problems and disease were common because of the poor conditions. In their book *Saddam Hussein: A Political Biography*, Efraim Karsh and Inari Rautsi state that "in an Iraqi village one of every two or three babies" died before reaching their first birthday, "mainly from infirmity and malnutrition."

Surviving the perils of disease and malnutrition did not guarantee anyone in Tikrit an easy life. In fact, Saddam Hussein's family life was as hard as the land around him. Saddam's father was a poor, landless peasant who disappeared from his life near the time of his birth. Some accounts say that Hussein's father died before he was born. Others simply say that he deserted the family. Whatever the truth may be, Saddam was left without a father. He was born in a mud hut belonging to his uncle, Khairallah Tulfah. Hussein's mother, Subha, faced with raising her child alone, left him with Tulfah and his family.

Family Ties

In Iraq, the idea of "family" is complex. Families are smaller parts of a greater network of clans and tribes that stretch across entire regions. These tribes often disagree with each other. They also have long histories of fighting and territorial struggles. Two of the largest groups in Iraq are the Sunni and the Shiite Muslims. About 60 percent of Iraq's 23 million people is Shiite. Twenty percent is Sunni, and 17 percent is Kurdish.

Saddam Hussein was born into the Sunni Muslim al-Bejat clan. The al-Bejat clan was a part of the larger

The Middle East

Iraq is nestled in the heart of a region of the world known as the Middle East. The Middle East has a rich and vibrant history full of great accomplishments. It is also a region of continuous conflict and turmoil. Many great contributions to the world's culture started in this area. People living on the banks of the Nile, Tigris, and Euphrates Rivers organized the first cities almost 5,000 years ago. Egypt is home to the pyramids. The religions of Judaism, Christianity, and Islam all began in this region. Arab mathematicians developed algebra, trigonometry, and geometry.

The Middle East is not an exact grouping of countries. Some historians disagree on the countries that compose this region. But almost everyone agrees that the Middle East consists of Egypt and all the countries surrounding the Persian Gulf. These include Lebanon, Israel, Syria, Jordan, Saudi Arabia, Yemen, Oman, the United Arab Emirates, Qatar, Bahrain, Kuwait, Iraq, and Iran.

Middle Eastern countries are often referred to as "Arab states." This means that the people of these countries speak Arabic as their first language. There are twenty-two Arab states in the Middle East and North Africa, including Iraq. These countries have a combined population of more than 200 million people.

The Middle East saddles Africa and Asia across the Red Sea in the west and the Persian Gulf in the east.

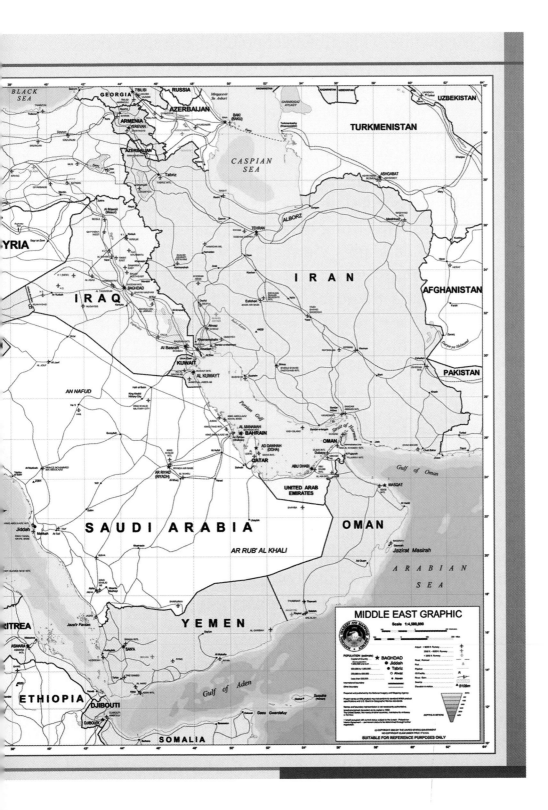

al-Bu Nasir tribe. This tribe held political and social power in most of the Tikrit region. The members of this clan were known for their grinding poverty and extreme acts of violence. Loyalty to one's own tribe is very important. When Hussein rose to power in Iraq, members from the Tikrit region soon held many government positions.

Khairallah Tulfah raised Saddam Hussein for several years. Many reports state that the young boy idolized his uncle. Tulfah held strong beliefs that may have begun to shape young Saddam's view of the world. Tulfah was a member of Iraq's armed forces. He strongly supported Adolf Hitler and the ideas of the Nazi Party. He was an Arab nationalist who dreamed that Arab countries in the Middle East would gain self-rule.

British forces controlled Iraq and occupied several military bases. Many Iraqis wanted them to leave. Hitler was gaining power, and World War II was on the horizon. Tulfah and many others believed that Germany would drive the British out of the Middle East. This would allow Iraq and other Arab states to become truly independent. In 1941, Tulfah joined an uprising against British forces. The attack failed, and he was soon expelled from the army and jailed for five years. With Tulfah in jail, Saddam was forced to return to his mother's house when he was four years old.

Hard Homecoming

What Saddam found at his mother's house in the village of al-Auja was the beginning of a nightmare that lasted for years. Saddam's mother, Subha, was a loud woman whose family photographs show her frowning darkly. Tribal tattoos dotted her cheeks. Subha had remarried

■ Hussein's rise to become leader of Iraq brought hope to many Iraqis. He promised a modernized country that would deal with the West as an equal, based on the Iraqi oil reserves that were needed by the world's industrial producers.

while Saddam was living with his uncle. Her new husband, Ibrahim Hassan, was known throughout the village as Hassan the Liar.

Hassan seemed to amuse himself by humiliating and abusing this young child who had come to live in his home. Hassan did not permit Saddam to attend school. Instead he sent Saddam to steal chickens and eggs from neighboring farms. Hassan often yelled insults at Saddam, calling him a "son of a dog." As punishment, Hassan beat Saddam with a stick covered with asphalt.

Pictures of Saddam Hussein as a child show haunting eyes beneath a crop of jet black hair. His eyebrows rise in a way that suggests worry and fear.

Saddam would often escape torture at the hands of his stepfather only to face further torment from the other boys in the village. They teased and mocked Saddam for being a fatherless child. In the Iraqi system of family honor, it is disgraceful to be without a father. The boys in the village did not only use words to attack Saddam. They also attacked him physically. These continued attacks and abuse stoked a building fire of rage, hurt, and anger within Saddam. It may be interesting to know that "Hussein" means "the one who confronts." Soon, Saddam Hussein began to live as his name suggested.

He began carrying an iron bar for defense against the village boys. One story about Saddam's early life shows how his anger was beginning to boil over. He placed the tip of his iron bar into a fire until it glowed red-hot. As a dog passed by, he stabbed the bar into its stomach, splitting the animal in half. Saddam was not even ten years old at the time.

Saddam received happy news when he was ten—his uncle Khairallah Tulfah had been released from prison. Saddam could finally escape the cruelty of his stepfather and the village boys. Tulfah had been permanently expelled from the Iraqi military. He now worked as a teacher at a local private school. His time in prison had hardened his views of the British presence in Iraq, and he often shared these views with whoever cared to listen. Tulfah had a son, Adnan Khairallah, who was three years younger than Hussein. Tulfah enrolled Saddam in school with Adnan, and the two quickly became close friends.

Schoolboy Hussein

Starting school was Saddam's first step toward education that was long overdue. But school presented its own problems. At ten years of age, Saddam could neither read nor write. He struggled to keep up with students who were half his age. Saddam relied on his streetwise ways to get him through. He was a clown and a practical joker in class to please his fellow students. This distracted attention from his struggles in the classroom. His jokes were not always innocent: He once slipped a snake into his teacher's robe while pretending to give him a friendly hug. On another occasion Saddam threatened to kill a headmaster who wanted to expel him from school. His threat worked. Saddam was not expelled.

After several years in school, Saddam's quick mind allowed him to catch up on his studies. Saddam proved to be an intelligent child who passed his classes but never excelled. Uncle Khairallah and Adnan encouraged him in his studies. Saddam dreamed of joining Iraq's army in the footsteps of his uncle.

Shortly before Saddam graduated from primary school, Tulfah got a new teaching job. This job took him far from the sleepy town of Tikrit with its dirt roads and lack of running water. His new job was in the heart of Iraq—the capital city of Baghdad.

Saddam and Adnan stayed in Tikrit to complete their studies. In 1955, Saddam graduated from primary school at the age of eighteen. Primary school in Iraq is the same as junior high school in the United States. Saddam wanted to fulfill his dream of joining the military. He applied to the Baghdad Military Academy in

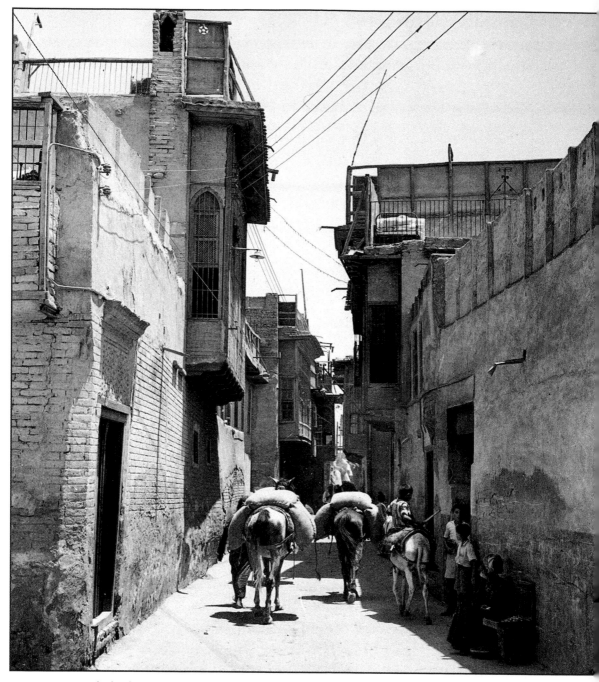

■ Baghdad, Iraq, was a small, dusty city in the middle of the twentieth century. Hussein came to the capital with high hopes. The bustling city offered many paths for the opportunistic young man.

Baghdad. He did not receive good news—his grades were not good enough. The military academy would not accept him.

Saddam was deeply disappointed, but his dreams of moving to Baghdad were not crushed. As soon as Saddam and Adnan graduated from school, they packed their bags and headed to Baghdad to live with Khairallah Tulfah. Leaving their little town behind, they soon discovered a big, beautiful, boisterous Baghdad. Saddam's move to Baghdad started a new direction that changed his life forever. One day the capital would be the home of Saddam Hussein's main presidential palace and the center of his own personal empire. His face would peer from city walls and every newspaper. Did Saddam dream of such power then? He was still a young man, and life was simple. It was time to go to high school.

CHAPTER TWO
LIFE IN BAGHDAD

■ The Shourga Bazaar in Baghdad brought together thousands of people every day. Shopping was just one activity people participated in at the bazaar. By the 1950s, Iraqi nationalism was strong. People met at the bazaar to discuss Iraqi nationalism and freedom from corrupt rulers.

When Saddam Hussein arrived in Baghdad, he discovered the capital city was unlike anything he had experienced before. Baghdad was a hive of activity and the center of the country's political movement.

Feelings of Arab nationalism were running high throughout the Middle East in 1955. Just three years before, an Egyptian army officer named Gamal Abdel Nasser had helped overthrow the ruling British monarchy in Egypt. After taking control of the country, Nasser then followed with several strong actions designed to drive Western countries out of the Middle East.

In 1955, Egypt purchased weapons from Czechoslovakia, a Soviet bloc country in Europe. The Soviet Union was then the greatest enemy of the West. Several months later, Nasser claimed the Suez Canal as the sole property of Egypt. The Suez was an important shipping route that had been constructed by France and was controlled by France and Britain. Britain and France attacked Egypt to regain control of the Suez Canal. When their attacks failed and Egypt kept the Suez, Nasser was hailed as a hero in the Arab world.

This wave of Arab pride swept through the Middle East. Baghdad was in the center of the storm. Many in Baghdad hoped that Iraq's monarchy would be the next to fall. King Faisal II had taken the throne of Iraq in 1953 at the young age of eighteen. It was widely believed that Faisal and his prime minister, Nuri Said, were too friendly with the West. The people of Baghdad were encouraged by Egypt's success in overthrowing a distasteful government. They began a rising tide of protests and resistance that often became violent. It didn't take long for Hussein to get swept up in the current. His life would never be the same.

A New Direction

The chaos and violence of street protests and political battles suited Hussein's personality. He seemed to

■ Pictured here are King Faisal II *(left)* and his uncle Prince Abdul Illah on the king's coronation day, May 2, 1953. People saw Faisal as a puppet of the West. Street protests put the king's rule in jeopardy when political protesters like Hussein incited violence.

thrive in this dog-eat-dog world. He found that he had a talent for organizing protests, often through intimidation. His childhood had taught him to use violence as a tool for survival.

The tension in Baghdad reached a breaking point in 1956. Angry mobs filled the streets. People from all walks of life demanded the overthrow of the Iraqi government. Hussein prowled through the crowds and seemed at home in this violent atmosphere. He had started high school with his cousin Adnan, but now found himself tempted by the country's growing political drama. He could not resist its seduction. Hussein left high school and plunged into this new and exciting world.

Hussein's political involvement allowed him to use his hate for people and brutality against all living things. Also adding to the flames was Khairallah Tulfah. Tulfah was a hateful man, too, and he groomed Hussein to follow in his footsteps. Tulfah wrote a pamphlet entitled *Three Whom God Should Not Have Created: Persians, Jews, and Flies*. In it he compares Jews to dirt and Iranians to animals. It is clear that Saddam Hussein respected and even shared his uncle's views. Years later, when Hussein assumed power in Iraq, he reprinted this pamphlet and distributed it throughout the country.

The Budding Politician

Hussein recognized that this game of power, manipulation, and violence was the perfect fit for him. He needed a political party into which he could channel his energies. He looked to Tulfah. With his help, Hussein found what he was looking for. Tulfah was involved with a small political party that expressed some radical views of Arab unity. Hussein must have liked what he heard. In 1957, at twenty years old, he joined the Baath Party.

The word "Baath" means "rebirth" or "renaissance" in Arabic. This describes the party's goal—to give birth to a new Arab world. The Baath Party began in 1940 as the idea of two schoolteachers in Syria. One was Christian and the other Muslim. Perhaps as a result, the Baath Party was not connected to any particular religion. The goal of Baathist members was to expel Western influences from their countries. The party's dream was a Middle East without foreign countries controlling its governments. In fact, party members dreamed of one unified Arab state that stretched from North Africa to Iraq. They wanted Arab countries to be run by the people, for the people. This idea was very popular in 1957 as people chanted in the streets for the overthrow of the Western-friendly Iraqi government. But the ranks of the Baath Party at that time were still small.

Hussein's reputation for violence and intimidation grew as he became more involved in the political world. At this point in his career, Hussein chose to speak mostly through his actions. He was quiet and kept to himself at most gatherings. When he did speak, his voice carried an accent from his rural upbringing in Tikrit. His rural Arabic marked him as an outsider in the slick urban landscape of Baghdad. Hussein's physical appearance overcame much of his early shyness. His body had developed into a powerful six-foot, two-inch frame. He could peer over most Iraqis in a crowd and stare down an opponent in a fight.

Behind Bars

Many people think that Saddam Hussein had already committed his first murder before his twentieth birthday. If so, he had never been arrested. But in 1958 that changed. Khairallah Tulfah had just been fired from a new job, and he was furious. He thought that he had been fired because of personal and political reasons. He believed a man named Saadoun al-Tikriti was responsible. Enraged, Tulfah ordered Hussein to take revenge. As al-Tikriti walked down a dark alley one night, a man stepped from the shadows and shot him in the head. Hussein was arrested for murder at the age of twenty-one. Tulfah was arrested also, and they were both thrown in jail.

Hussein and Tulfah spent six months in prison. They kept to themselves, staying in a corner of their cell and rarely mingling with the other prisoners. After six months, they were released for lack of evidence. Once more Hussein was on the streets. And now he had a reputation as someone who would kill for his job. This made him more valuable to the Baath Party. They were looking for someone to commit an important assassination. In fact, they wanted to kill the ruler of Iraq.

Assassin

General Abdul Karim Qasim had risen to power in 1958. As a military officer and Arab nationalist, he resented Iraq's monarchy and wished for self-rule. Leading a group of other military personnel who called themselves the Free Officers (named after Nasser's group that took control of Egypt), he made a grab for power. The officers

Saddam Hussein

■ Iraqi prime minister Abdul Karim Qasim fell out of favor with the nationalist Baath Party. Hussein was part of a team chosen to assassinate Qasim. The assassins failed, and Hussein had to flee the country. Hussein became a hero among Baathist sympathizers.

assassinated King Faisal II in a bloody coup, and Qasim was named the new ruler of Iraq. Relations between Qasim and the Baath Party were good at first, but they soon soured. The Baath Party wanted him out of power. Baath leaders chose Hussein as a member of a five-man assassination team.

Hussein and the other men planned to ambush Qasim as he drove home from work. They knew that only a few bodyguards traveled with Qasim. The plan was simple: three men would provide covering gunfire while two shot Qasim at close range. Hussein was supposed to provide covering fire once the main assassins made their move. But it didn't work out that way. It seems that Hussein got nervous—or maybe excited—as the car approached.

He pulled his gun and started shooting before the assassins got a clear shot. Qasim's bodyguards dove into position to protect him as he crouched on the car floor. Hussein killed the driver and wounded a bodyguard, but the plan rapidly unraveled. The members of the assassin team fired their bullets wildly and began shooting each other by accident. The leader of the squad was killed. Hussein and another man were also wounded. The plan had turned to chaos, and the assassins ran for their lives.

Even though the assassination failed, this event was a major turning point for both Hussein and the Baath Party. General Qasim publicly demanded the arrest of his would-be assassins. Hussein was suddenly a national figure, and the Baath Party was one to be feared. Stories of the assassination attempt grew wilder with each telling, and Hussein himself told some of the most colorful tales.

According to Hussein's own account, he was wounded seriously by a bullet to the leg. He tried to seek medical treatment but was refused. A comrade then cut the bullet out with a razor blade as he bravely sat and endured the pain. Another version of the story says that Hussein used his own knife to dig the bullet out, then galloped on his horse across the desert toward Syria. When his horse reached the Tigris River, Hussein jumped into the water and swam across with a knife clenched between his teeth.

What really happened? The truth may never be known. In *Hussein: King of Terror,* author Con Coughlin says that the doctor who treated Hussein's wounds observed "nothing more than a flesh wound really, a graze." But Hussein was already learning the power of propaganda, and he built a bungled murder attempt into a story of his own heroism. He was now one of the most wanted criminals in Iraq. What is known for sure is that Hussein escaped the country before the police could find him. He fled to Syria, where he began his life in exile.

■ Hussein's lust for violence was known about early in his career. In this photograph, he speaks to a crowd on the occasion of the hanging of fourteen Iraqis. The executed men had been charged with spying for Israel.

Life in Exile

Hussein found that Syria welcomed him with open arms. Michel Aflaq, one of the founders of the Baath Party, received Hussein and applauded his efforts. After three months in Syria, Hussein moved to Egypt. It was time to finish high school.

As in Syria, Hussein found that his presence was welcomed. Nasser himself protected Hussein. Hussein received an allowance from the Egyptian government that supported him while he attended school. Hussein enrolled in high school in Cairo, Egypt's capital city. In 1961, at the age of twenty-four, he graduated.

Hussein received protection while in Egypt, but his heart remained in Iraq. Iraq's government had sentenced Hussein to fifteen years in prison if he ever returned to Iraqi soil. Hussein knew that his only hope of returning to his homeland was the overthrow of Qasim's government. Several years dragged by. Hussein watched and waited, and planned for his return.

It is clear that Hussein fully expected to return to Iraq. While still exiled in Egypt, he asked to marry the daughter of his uncle Khairallah Tulfah. Sajida was two years older than he was. A marriage to his uncle's daughter would show Hussein's allegiance to Tulfah and strengthen family ties. Tulfah agreed to the marriage. With his future wife in Baghdad, Hussein could only sit and wait.

After three years in exile, Hussein finally got the news he had been waiting for. In 1963, a group of Baath Army (a non-state-supported political/guerrilla group) officers killed Qasim. The Baath Party now ruled Iraq, and Saddam Hussein could return to his homeland.

CHAPTER THREE
BAATH TAKEOVER

■ Hussein (right) is shown here in a rare photo with Baathist leaders. The Baathist politicians thought Hussein a crude man who lacked political savvy. He did well as a security strongman, however, a job he got with the help of his uncle.

Saddam Hussein came home to a new regime in Baghdad. The overthrow of Qasim had been brutal and bloody. Baath Party soldiers paraded pictures of Qasim's corpse on television to prove his death. Iraqi citizens watched as a soldier displayed the bullet holes that riddled the ruler's body. This cruelty and violence was a hint of things to come from Hussein and the workings of the Baath Party.

After his three-year exile in Egypt, Hussein was out of touch with the inner workings of the Iraqi Baath Party. He wanted political power, but many top leaders did not consider him to be an impressive figure. Hussein's coarse accent did not distinguish him as a polished speaker. His reputation for violence also singled him out as more of a party thug than a leader. He needed a lucky break. He soon got one.

General Ahmad Hassan al-Bakr was the new prime minister of Iraq. Al-Bakr was one of Hussein's older cousins and a native of Tikrit. These strong family ties assured Hussein a place in the new government.

Hussein the Strongman

The job that al-Bakr chose for Hussein was a dark and violent task that continued the horrors of the Baath takeover. He was in charge of interrogation and torture. Hussein seemed to enjoy this task. He was ruthlessly efficient. Squads of his interrogators combed the streets of Baghdad, arresting thousands

■ Baathist leaders Hardan Tikriti, Ahmad Hassan Al-Bakr, and Hammad Chehab fell from power after only nine months in 1963. They hid from police for nearly a year before returning to power. Iraqi leadership changed hands again before the Baathists took total control in 1969.

of people who posed a threat to the new regime. Hundreds were killed by brutal torture. Some prisoners were dropped into vats of acid. Others were whipped with lengths of hose filled with stones. Hussein set up this shop of horrors in the palace where King Faisal II had been overthrown many years before. It was known as the Palace of the End. The name fit. Many prisoners did not leave alive.

Fortunately for the Iraqi people, this reign of terror lasted less than a year. Political divisions within the Baath Party weakened its hold on the country. Just nine months into the new regime, a group of military officers overthrew the Baath Party. The Baath Party was declared illegal by the new government, and Baath members were forced to hide from the police.

On the Run Again

Hussein was a fugitive from the law once again, but this time he did not leave the country. The members of the Baath Party were determined to regain power. In 1964, Ahmad Hassan al-Bakr regained the top leadership position of the Iraqi Baath Party. He placed Hussein in charge

■ Hussein's public appearances portrayed a leader of the people. Here he welcomes a Kurdistani leader, Mulla Mustafa al-Barzani. Behind the scenes, however, Hussein proved to be a lover of torture and murder.

of security operations. Hussein approached his task with gusto.

Hussein formed a secret police force called the Jihaz Haneen, or "Instrument of Yearning." The importance of family ties was very clear. All of the members were from Tikrit, and most were related to Hussein by blood or marriage. This band of thugs and killers began wiping out anyone who posed a threat to al-Bakr's return to power. Some people disappeared without a trace. Hussein was beginning to perfect his blend of terror and intimidation to secure political power.

Family Man

Hussein did not hesitate to tear apart families through these brutal methods. But even as he killed the sons and daughters of Iraqi citizens, he was starting a family of his own. Hussein's first son was born on June 18, 1964. Hussein and his wife, Sajida, named him Uday.

Hussein spent only a few short months with his newborn son. In October 1964, the government's security forces caught up with Hussein and threw him in jail. They charged him with conspiring to overthrow the government. This time he was determined not to lose touch with the powerful members of the Baath Party, as he had in Egypt. When Sajida came to visit with baby Uday, Hussein slipped letters into Uday's clothing. Sajida then delivered the notes to al-Bakr. Al-Bakr delivered notes to Hussein in the same manner.

Hussein spent two years in jail. In 1966, he escaped from two guards who were taking him to the court-house. Hussein was on the run once again. By now, though, he was an expert at living outside the law. He

■ Sajida Hussein, wife of Saddam, posed for a photograph in 1989. She bore Hussein two sons and three daughters during their marriage. It's hard to imagine that early in their marriage she did not know of her husband's murderous deeds performed against Iraqis.

simply disappeared into the folds of the Baath Party. He moved from house to house, staying with friends and evading arrest. This was a tactic he would later use in the first Persian Gulf War in 1991.

Another Overthrow

Hussein reunited with al-Bakr, and they began planning another government overthrow. The time was ripe for political change. In 1967, a coalition of Arab countries was soundly defeated by Israel. In an event known today as the Six-Day War, Israel crushed a combined army from Egypt, Jordan, and Syria. Iraq sent only a small contingent of soldiers. The Israeli army occupied the Sinai Peninsula, the Gaza Strip, the Golan Heights (on Israel's border with Syria), the West Bank (on Israel's border with Jordan), and East Jerusalem in one dramatic sweep. The Arab nations were stunned. Many Iraqis thought that Iraq should have sent more soldiers into the conflict. They blamed their government for making the wrong decision.

Hussein and al-Bakr saw their chance to weaken Iraq's ruling regime. The Baath Party quickly organized antigovernment protests and demonstrations in the streets. They called for the overthrow of President Abdul Rahma Arif, a weak ruler who enjoyed little popular support. At the same time they began looking for supporters in Arif's own military forces. By 1968, they found the support they needed. Colonel Abd ar-Razzaq an-Nayif was head of military intelligence. Colonel Abd ar-Rahman ad-Daud was commander of the Republican Guard (specially trained soldiers who protect the capital city). Both men promised to help

■ Iraq's involvement in the 1967 Six-Day War against Israel was small. The country sent only a small band of troops and weaponry. The Arab forces' defeat at the hands of Israel helped to weaken the Iraqi regime. The Baathists used the occasion to take full and final control of Iraq.

overthrow President Arif and restore the Baath Party to power.

The July Revolution

On July 17, 1968, the trap was set. Baath forces surrounded the president's palace in the middle of the night. A phone call woke the sleeping president. A voice on the line calmly informed him that the Baath Party had taken over the country. Hussein, dressed in army clothing, sat atop a tank that rumbled into the president's courtyard. President Arif had little choice but to step down.

The Power of the Purge

Adolf Hitler in 1937 addressing a meeting of the National Socialist Party (Nazis)

Most people shudder when they think of past dictators like Adolf Hitler and Josef Stalin. Hitler's persecution of Jews, Christians, Gypsies, and other "undesirables" in Germany left more than 6 million people dead. Stalin killed up to 20 million people in Russia as he tried to create the perfect Communist state. History views these men with revulsion, but Hussein viewed them as teachers. From them he learned the power of the purge. The selective targeting and elimination of political enemies and ethnic groups mark Hussein's earliest days in politics.

His own forces had deserted him. Within hours he was flown to London in exile.

Thankfully for the Iraqi people, the coup was peaceful. But the Baath Party was in power for good this time, and Hussein was working his way up the ladder of political power. The coming years would be anything but peaceful.

Once again the Iraqi people had a new government ruling them. President Al-Bakr moved quickly to establish the new power structure. He named himself prime minister of Iraq and commander in chief of the armed forces. Khairallah Tulfah was named mayor of Baghdad. Many other Tikritis also received government positions. The family web of power from Tikrit was now ruling the entire country. And the most important Tikriti besides al-Bakr was Saddam Hussein himself. Al-Bakr personally picked Hussein to be the deputy chairman of the Revolutionary Command Council. The details of his new job were familiar. He was once again in charge of security for the new regime.

Secret Hussein

Hussein was now the second most powerful man in the country. He was second in command to President al-Bakr. More important, he was al-Bakr's close personal friend and adviser. Despite his new power, Hussein chose to keep a low profile for the first year in office. Few outside Iraq even knew who he was. Part of the reason for this is that Hussein kept his appointment a secret. He publicly refused to take an official government position. Hussein's reason for this was probably very practical— he did not want to be a target. And he wanted a chance to clear away any opposition to the Baath Party without attracting too much attention. Behind the scenes, he was a very busy man.

A now familiar pattern emerged once Hussein went to work. His security forces began ferocious purges of any opposition to the Baath Party. Hussein targeted members of the military so that they could not pose a threat to the Baath regime. Rising stars in the political world were killed or simply disappeared. Hussein exposed supposed plots and executed the accused. In January 1969, he killed fourteen Jews whom he called an "Israeli ring of spies." They were lynched in the public square in Baghdad. Angry mobs danced around the bodies, and 200,000 Iraqis came to see the spectacle.

People within the Baath Party were also systematically targeted, then killed or exiled. President al-Bakr wanted a strongman to secure the Baath Party's hold on power, and Hussein was the perfect henchman. But within a decade, al-Bakr would be a target in Hussein's merciless quest for power.

After a year in office, Hussein chose to publicly acknowledge his position as deputy chairman. But he still made an effort to appear humble and respectful of his place in the new government. In government circles he was addressed simply as Mr. Deputy. In truth, Hussein was biding his time and building his power.

CHAPTER FOUR

SEIZING POWER

■ The Soviet defense minister, General Andrei Grechko, met with Hussein, serving as the Iraqi minister of interior, at a 1971 conference. Hussein dressed as a modern politician while in public. Already he was working his way up the Baathist political ladder.

Hussein appeared humble in public, but in private he had found a taste for high living. He bought expensive suits custom made by Iraq's finest tailors. Mercedes limousines whisked him smoothly from one

Saddam Hussein

■ A private family photo shows the extended family of Saddam Hussein. The two men dressed in military uniform are sons-in-law of the Iraqi dictator. They were both murdered by Hussein after defecting to the West and then returning in 1999.

location to the next. Hussein dined on American-style food, such as spare ribs. He also began puffing on expensive cigars. For relaxation he enjoyed hunting pheasant with other Baath Party members. He began buying land outside of Baghdad to build homes for himself in all corners of Iraq. Eventually, fourteen palaces were built throughout the country. By 1972, Hussein was the father of three daughters and two sons. The family lived together on the grounds of the presidential palace in a house with swimming pools and hired servants. He was only thirty-five years old, and the future looked bright. The peasant boy from Tikrit had come a long way.

Tightening His Grip

In the 1970s, Hussein gradually increased his role in the government until he was making many of the day-to-day decisions for the country. By 1975, Hussein controlled almost every aspect of Iraqi policy. The shy and calculating young man had grown into a handsome and confident leader. Hussein's bright smile graced the living room of almost every Iraqi citizen. Pictures of Hussein covered the daily newspapers and many walls in the city. State-controlled television showed scenes of Hussein with his wife and children. They were the picture of a perfect Iraqi family.

He was a growing presence on the international scene as well. He received heads of state from foreign countries and handled high-profile visitors. In 1975, Hussein moved to stop the Kurdish uprising in northern Iraq. He signed the Algiers Agreement with Iran, in which Iraq conceded land on the strategically important Shatt al-Arab waterway. In exchange, Iran stopped assisting the Kurds. In 1977, Hussein appointed his cousin Adnan Khairallah as minister of defense. With friends and family in prominent positions, Hussein knew that his grip on power was safer than ever before.

Hussein now controlled almost every aspect of Iraq except for one: He was still not the president. Hussein had needed al-Bakr's support in the early days of the regime, but now time had run out. Al-Bakr was getting old, and Hussein felt the aging president was unable to continue his duties. Saddam Hussein was ready to take control.

Oil, Money, and Mass Destruction

President Saddam Hussein inherited a country on a powerful surge of growth, wealth, and opportunity. Money was pouring into Iraq from the sale of its huge oil reserves. Iraq contains 11 percent of the world's oil reserves (proven oil reserves equal 113 billion barrels). Only Saudi Arabia has more. Several foreign countries had controlled Iraq's oil fields until 1972. As a result, much of Iraq's oil wealth ended up in the pockets of European powers. In one of his first major political victories, Hussein helped Iraq nationalize the oil industry in 1972. Once Iraq regained control of its own resources, revenues began to pour in.

This river of oil and the money that came with it turned Iraq into an international power. Western countries were eager to do business with this new oil giant in the Middle East. Hussein funneled money into modernization projects throughout the country. He sent doctors and other professionals to study in Europe and return with the latest knowledge. He built new schools and spearheaded a nationwide literacy program. It appeared that Hussein was creating a new empire in the Middle East that shared many Western values.

But hints of Hussein's future plans soon began to surface. Oil dollars were also feeding a growing weapons program. Military spending increased from $500 million in 1970 to $4.5 billion in 1975. Hussein began purchasing materials to create chemical and biological weapons as early as 1974. By 1979, Iraq was poised to begin a full-scale nuclear weapons program with a nuclear reactor purchased from France. By the time of the First Gulf War in 1991, Iraq's military was the fourth largest in the world.

Iraq used revenue from its huge oil reserves *(top left)* to build biological weapons facilities *(top right)*, nuclear weapons research sites *(bottom right)*, and a rocket program *(bottom left)*.

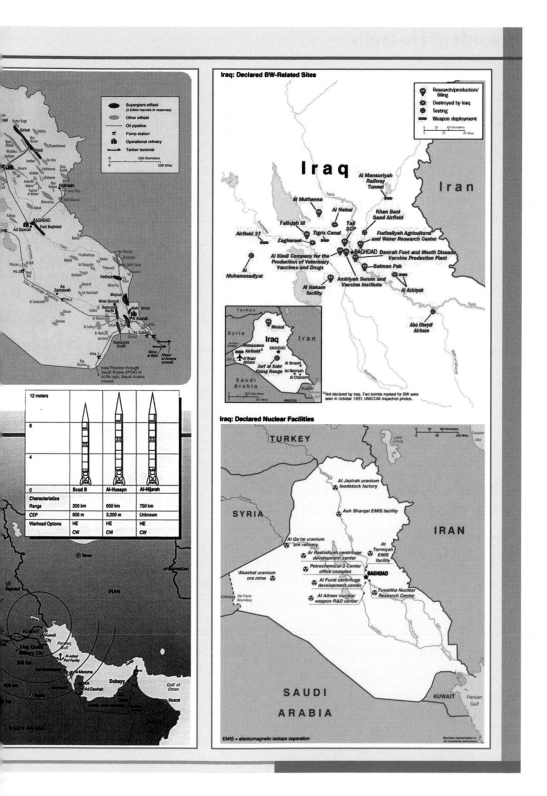

Iraq: Declared BW-Related Sites

Research/production/
filling
Destroyed by Iraq
Testing
Weapon deployment

Iraq

Iran

Al Mansuriyah
Railway
Tunnel

Al Muthanna

Al Nebai

Khan Bani
Saad Airfield

Falluiah III

Taji
SCP

Fudhaliyah Agricultural
and Water Research Center

Airfield 37

Tigris Canal

Zagharest

Dawrah Foot and Mouth Disease
Vaccine Production Plant

Al Kindi Company for the
Production of Veterinary
Vaccines and Drugs

BAGHDAD

Salman Pak

Muhaimmadiyat

Amiriyah Serum and
Vaccine Institute

Al Hakam
facility

Al Aziziyah

Abu Obeydi
Airbase

Turkey

Mosul

Syria

Iraq

BAGHDAD

Khurasana
Airfield

Iran

Al 'Amariya

Al Wakil
Airbase

Jurf al Sakr
Firing Range

An Nasiriyah

Al Chabanis

Saudi
Arabia

Kuwait

*Not declared by Iraq. Two bombs marked for BW were
seen in October 1991 UNSCOM inspection photos.

Iraq: Declared Nuclear Facilities

TURKEY

Lake
Urmia

Al Jazirah uranium
feedstock factory

SYRIA

Ash Sharqat EMIS facility

IRAN

Al Qa'im uranium
ore refinery

At
Tarmiyah
EMIS
facility

Ar Rashidiyah centrifuge
development center

Petrochemical-3 Center
office complex

BAGHDAD

'Akashat uranium
ore mine

Al Furat centrifuge
development center

Tuwaitha Nuclear
Research Center

JORDAN

De-Facto
Boundary

Al Atheer nuclear
weapon R&D center

SAUDI

ARABIA

KUWAIT

Persian
Gulf

EMIS = electromagnetic isotope separation

Boundary representation is
not necessarily authoritative.

Supergiant oilfield
(5 billion barrels in reserves)
Other oilfield
Oil pipeline
Pump station
Operational refinery
Tanker terminal

100 Kilometers

100 Miles

Kirkuk

BAGHDAD
East Baghdad
Ad Dawrah

As Samawah

West Qurnah

Ramaylah
North

Al Basrah

At Zubayr

Ramaylah
South

Minn
al Bakr

Khawr
al Amaya
(closed)

Iraq's Pipeline through
Saudi Arabia (IPSA) to
Al Mu'ajiz, Saudi Arabia
(closed)

12 meters			
8			
4			
0	Scud B	Al-Husayn	Al-Hijarah
Characteristics			
Range	300 km	600 km	750 km
CEP	900 m	3,000 m	Unknown
Warhead Options	HE	HE	HE
	CW	CW	CW

Tehran

AFGHANISTAN

IRAN

Baghdad

KUWAIT
Kuwait
City

King Khalid
Military City

Persian
Gulf

Al-Jubayl
Port Facility

300 km

Ad-Dammam

Al-Manama

Dubayy

Gulf of
Oman

600 km

Ad-Dawhah

Muscat

Riyadh

SAUDI ARABIA

President Hussein

On July 16, 1979, President al-Bakr appeared on Iraqi television for the last time. He informed the Iraqi people that he was stepping down as their leader. He reassured the country that they would be in capable hands under the leadership of his comrade Saddam Hussein. As al-Bakr read this message, Hussein was being sworn in as the new president of Iraq. Al-Bakr was almost certainly forced from power by Hussein and his closest henchmen. This was Hussein's ultimate achievement in his life so far. He was now the president of Iraq and only forty-two years old.

Hussein Sets the Tone

Within a week Hussein set the tone for his new regime. The people knew Hussein already as the leader of Iraq. But Hussein wanted everyone to know that resistance to his rule was futile. He sent the message to the people through brutal purges and terror tactics. Almost immediately he began cleansing the country of supposed spies and lurking terrorists. Thousands of innocent Iraqis disappeared, never to be seen again.

But Hussein wasn't only worried about an uprising from the ranks of the common people of Iraq. He knew firsthand that members of the military and often the ruling party itself had carried out recent government overthrows. He needed a way to erase any enemies within his own party. Hussein summoned a meeting of the Revolutionary Command Council on July 22, 1979. Just less than a week had passed since he had taken power. The highest Baath Party officials filed into an

■ By 1975, Saddam Hussein controlled much of the day-to-day operations of running the Iraqi government. He had achieved this through family connections, his leadership in the secret police, and political intimidation. No one in the Baath Party was willing to risk his life by opposing Hussein.

auditorium and sat down. A guard in the rear of the hall captured the entire event on videotape. Here is how the scene plays out:

Hussein lounges in an armchair like a relaxed lion. A cigar rests in his hands. As the audience watches, Taha Yassin Ramadan, a Baath Party member, comes to the podium. He announces that a massive conspiracy has been discovered within the Baath Party—a conspiracy to overthrow the government. To the astonishment of those in the audience, he says that the other conspirators are present in the auditorium. As proof, he calls a Baath member named Mashhadi to the front. Mashhadi confesses that he had been part of this wide-ranging plot. He lists dates and locations of secret meetings. He then moves aside to make way for Hussein.

Hussein steps to the podium with the confidence of a seasoned actor. After a few remarks he begins to read a list of names. The tension rises to an unbearable level as Hussein calls out the names on his list of "conspirators." Each name identifies a different man in the audience. Many men break down in tears as they sit in their seats, praying that their names will not be called. Hussein seems to enjoy the moment and occasionally stops to puff on his cigar. As Hussein calls each name, his security forces usher that person from the room. What awaits them is an almost certain death sentence. A total of sixty-six men are led from the room. Some of Hussein's closest friends and colleagues—at least, they had thought they had been—are led away.

On August 8, twenty-two of the men were killed by "democratic executions." The accused men knelt on the ground with their hands tied behind their backs.

Hussein invited senior Baath Party officials to execute their own former friends and colleagues. He provided a pistol to each "executioner" and personally participated in the bloodbath that followed. Once again, a guard captured the proceedings on video. Copies of the video were soon sent to surviving Baath members and even leaders of neighboring Arab countries. His message was clear—Iraq was Hussein's country now. And all the Baath Party members had blood on their hands.

CHAPTER FIVE
THE IRAN-IRAQ WAR

■ Armed women guard one of the main squares in Tehran, Iran, at the beginning of the Iranian Revolution in 1979. Hussein would use Iranian instability to launch an attack on the neighboring country. The attack was launched as a land grab that would yield Iran's rich oil fields.

With his own country in order, Hussein took stock of the situation in the Middle East. Looking beyond Iraq's border, Hussein had reason for concern. Iraq's neighbor Iran was in the midst of a revolution that threatened to sweep through Iraq and the Middle East. In 1979, the people of Iran rose up and overthrew the ruling shah, a ruler friendly to the West who seemed out of touch with the needs of his people. In his place now stood the Ayatollah Khomeini, who ushered in an era of Islamic fundamentalism. Iran's Shiite Muslims started calling for the overthrow of Saddam Hussein, inspired by their new leader.

Hussein the Shiite

Shiites in Iraq far outnumbered the Sunnis, and Hussein was worried. He resorted to familiar tactics—propaganda and purges. In 1979, Hussein went on a publicity spree designed to win over the hearts and minds of Iraqi Shiites. He visited Shiite towns, dressed in traditional clothes, and handed out televisions as gifts. In a bizarre sign of his desperation, he produced a family tree that "proved" he was descended from the prophet Muhammad. When that failed to convince people, he executed hundreds of Shiite leaders and expelled almost 80,000 Shiites from the country. Resistance was still stiff, however, and Hussein remained worried.

Western powers were worried too. They feared that the ayatollah's wave of Islamic fundamentalism would spread across the Middle East. Ayatollah Khomeini openly opposed the West. Western businesses had millions of dollars invested in oil fields in the Middle East, and they didn't want to lose that money. Given the choice between the ayatollah and Hussein, they chose Hussein. They saw him as the lesser of two evils. Stories of Hussein's cruelty had already reached Western powers, but they chose to look the other way. Hussein seemed to

◼ Hussein once again played the role of the fatherly leader at the outset of his war with Iran. Here he meets with troops before they go off to battle. They believed that glory would come to them in war.

be a much smaller threat to their flow of oil and money.

Picking a Fight

Iraq and Iran began disputing the rights to the Shatt al-Arab waterway, an important trading route that Iran had controlled since the 1975 Algiers Agreement. This issue became the "official" reason for the increasing tensions between the two countries. Hussein wanted to negotiate the rights to the Shatt al-Arab waterway to get a better trading position. He also wanted to show his dominance over Iran's new government in order to subdue the rumblings in his own country.

Ayatollah Khomeini soon increased the pressure on Hussein. On June 8, 1980, the ayatollah publicly urged Iraqi Shiites to overthrow what he called "Hussein's Government." The 1,000-mile (1,609 km) border between Iraq and Iran heated up with military skirmishes and gun battles.

Neighbors at War

On September 17, 1980, Hussein pledged to bring the Shatt al-Arab waterway under Iraqi control. Five days later, Iraq plunged into war. Iraqi aircraft screamed through the sky on

Nuclear Nightmare?

A large poster of Ayatollah Ruhollah Khomeini, leader of Iran, is plastered over the mosaics in a mosque.

Iran tried to bomb Iraq's nuclear reactor one week into the war and failed. Everyone in the region feared the threat of nuclear war. Another Middle Eastern neighbor got involved. On June 7, 1981, the Israeli air force destroyed the reactor. Hussein's nuclear program came to a screeching halt, and the region breathed a sigh of relief.

the morning of September 22 and attacked ten Iranian air bases. Perhaps Hussein was really concerned with the importance of the waterway. But he was most likely trying to save his own skin.

The decision to go to war with Iran was the first step in a long decline that would take Iraq from the top of the Arab world to the depths of chaos and anarchy. Hussein may have been skilled at ruling a country by terror, but he was certainly not a military expert. This was Hussein's big chance to lead troops into battle and fulfill his dream of being a great military commander. But there is probably a good reason that the Baghdad Military Academy rejected Hussein. Many critics claim that Hussein bungled his attempts at military leadership and plunged his country into a war that could not be won.

Hussein expected Iran to fold without a struggle. He insisted that Iraqis should go about their lives as usual. The war would be over soon, and the Iraqi people shouldn't have to change their routines. Hussein sorely underestimated the power of the ayatollah's religious fire. Ayatollah Khomeini convinced Iranian fighters that they were assured a spot in heaven by dying in battle. Thousands of willing recruits stormed Iraqi positions, day after day. Forty-five thousand Iraqi troops died in the first two months of battle. France and other Western countries were supplying Iraq with the latest military technology. The United States supplied military information and satellite photos revealing Iranian troop positions. Persian Gulf states funneled money to Iraq to aid the battle against the Iranian threat. None of this proved enough, though, to turn back the waves of Iranian suicide fighters.

Shifting Hussein

Saddam Hussein was a political chameleon. His main concern was survival rather than a commitment to any ideals. During the war with Iran, he realized the power of motivating his people through religion. The Baath Party had not been founded on any religious principles, but Hussein soon soaked his speeches in religious images. The selections below show how much Hussein changed his message in the course of ten years.

From a 1980 interview (p. 31, *Hussein Reader*)

"Although we may be inspired by religion and its laws, we do not deal with life by following a religious path . . . We do not believe in dealing with life through religion because it would not serve the Arab nation."

Speech to Iraqi people, September 5, 1990 (pp. 239–240, *Hussein Reader*)

"In the name of God, the merciful, the compassionate. O great Iraqi people, O faithful Arabs wherever you may be, O Muslims in our Islamic world . . . Almighty God has chosen the Arab homeland as the field of confrontation and the Arabs as the leaders of the faithful gathering with the Iraqis as the vanguard force."

The War Drags On . . . and On

The Iran-Iraq War dragged on day after day, year after year. Iraq's economy slowed to a crawl as men and boys were sent to the battlefront. The jolly family man whom Iraqis had observed on television had begun to show a different side. In 1986, Hussein passed a decree that threatened the death penalty for anyone who insulted the president. Anyone who joked about Hussein or any aspect of the Baath Party could be arrested, imprisoned, and killed. Citizens were encouraged to report anyone who violated this law. This turned people within the country against each other and strengthened Hussein's position. No one dared to speak out against Hussein. How could you talk with your neighbors if they might report you to the police?

Hussein the Builder

As ordinary citizens absorbed the impact of war in the 1980s, Hussein began a personal building spree. He built magnificent palaces in every corner of the country at a cost of up to $500 million apiece. Each palace had its own orchard and vegetable gardens for a steady food supply. The walls were built strong enough to absorb missile attacks. Some had private zoos holding lions, tigers, antelope, and alligators. A full staff of personal servants and chefs took care of each home. As a security measure, three meals were prepared every day in each of Hussein's palaces. This was designed to confuse anyone who tried to observe the leader's movements. Since each palace had the same bustle of activity, you could never tell whether Hussein was staying there. Hussein never stayed in one place for long and moved among his palaces. Some of them were never used.

Cease-fire

The Iran-Iraq War finally ended in 1988 when Iran agreed to a cease-fire. Both countries had exhausted

■ The port of Khorramshahr in Iraq was the scene of heavy fighting during Iraq's eight-year battle with Iran. While his troops fought and died for Iraqi-Muslim pride, Hussein built himself lush palaces and dined on Western food.

themselves in the eight-year war. Iraq was certainly a different place now. The country was nearly drained of its former wealth because little oil had been sold during the war years. The people had paid a high cost. More than 200,000 Iraqi men and boys had been killed. Twice as many carried injuries that would be with them until their deaths. Hussein claimed victory for Iraq, but few believed him, or agreed. The boundaries of Iran and Iraq remained the same.

CHAPTER SIX
THE FIRST GULF WAR

■ Ethnic Kurds in the north of Iraq felt the wrath of Saddam Hussein in 1988. Mustard gas bombs like the one shown above were dropped on dozens of Kurdish villages. Thousands lay dead in the streets after the attacks.

Iraq's fragile balance threatened to topple. Hussein hoped that things would improve now that the war was over. Unfortunately, they only got worse. Ethnic Kurds in northern Iraq rose up in revolt against Hussein's government. Hussein's response was quick and brutal. In 1988, his troops attacked sixty-five Kurdish villages in the northern mountains with chemical weapons.

In an attack that attracted international attention, his military commander Ali Hassan al-Majid bombarded the Kurdish village of Halabja with mustard gas. More than 5,000 Kurds lay dead in the streets. Most of the victims were women and children. This terrifying attack earned the commander the nickname Chemical Ali. Kurds scattered into the countryside, fleeing for their lives. Some 100,000 Kurds ran for Turkey and Iran to find safety. Some made it, while others were captured by Iraqi troops. Kurdish women were sent to detention camps, where they were often raped. The men simply disappeared. There is little doubt that they were executed. Turkey and Iran sheltered 250,000 refugees within a year after the attacks began.

The World Reacts, Sort Of

There was no question now that Hussein was capable of terrible acts. Countries across the world raised cries of anger and criticism. The United States Congress and the European community publicly considered sanctions against Iraq. But Iraq was still seen as a powerful trading partner and potential ally in the Persian Gulf region. Besides, the West was still more scared of Iran than Iraq. Despite the public criticism, the international community was very soft on Hussein. It basically let him off with a promise—he agreed to stop using chemical weapons. This was not even a slap on the wrist for a man who had just devastated an entire region with chemical weapons.

The Price of Power

A torture room ready for Hussein's enemies

Power has its price. As Hussein created his own empire, he also created his own prison. Fearful of any plot or threat to his power, Hussein tightened the controls on every aspect of his life. Visitors were stripped and searched before seeing the president. He rarely shook hands for fear of contracting germs. His food was flown in from all over the world. Before any food reached his table, it was sent to his nuclear scientists for X-rays and poison tests. He refused to eat in public, fearing the possibility of being poisoned.

The daily life of this dictator was no picnic. Hussein maintained strict personal discipline. He was known for keeping a tough work schedule. Advisers sometimes saw a cot in Hussein's office where he had slept the night before. After sleeping only five or six hours a night, he worked twelve to fourteen hours a day. He rose as early as 3 AM for a morning swim in one of his numerous pools.

This episode reminded Hussein that he was in a fragile position. He could not afford international criticism at such a vulnerable time. The standard of living in Iraq had plummeted, and the economy was battered from eight years of fighting. The powerful country that had entered the war in 1980 was now saddled with $80 billion in foreign debts. Iraq owed half of that to the Arab states in the Persian Gulf. Hussein now needed the support of Arab neighbors like Saudi Arabia and Kuwait. This was hard to swallow for a leader who did not trust anyone. His political mind went into high gear. Iraq was now dependent on others for help, and Hussein set out to make the most of the situation.

A New Hussein?

To the people of Iraq and other countries of the world, it soon appeared that Hussein was steering Iraq in a new direction. He began to relax some of the restrictions in the political system. Hussein promised to establish a multiparty political system and hold general elections. Iraqi newspapers began printing stories from citizens of their hardships and complaints about daily life. Western reporters were flown in to observe these new signs of democracy. Members of the Arab press were also invited and treated to lavish dinners and given fancy cars to use.

On the international stage, Hussein positioned Iraq as the new leader and protector of the Arab world. With President Hosni Mubarak of Egypt, Iraq officially acknowledged Israel's state rights. He improved Iraq's relations with Jordan and other Arab countries. In February 1989, Hussein played a key role in the formation of the Arab Cooperation Council (ACC). The ACC was an alliance between Egypt, North Yemen, Jordan, and Iraq. A month later Iraq also signed a nonaggression pact with Saudi Arabia.

Little did his own people, the region, and the world know that these moves were nothing more than an image makeover and an attempt to strengthen Iraq's position in a time of weakness. And they worked. In every situation in life, Hussein turned circumstances to his own advantage. Western powers took the bait and began pouring money into Iraq. They were encouraged by Hussein's verbal support of Israel and hoped that he would become a force for good in the region. France had supported Iraq during the war with weapons and loans. That close relationship continued. In 1990, Britain became Iraq's third largest trade partner. The United States provided Iraq with a $1 billion agricultural credit. This was the largest agricultural loan in the world to any single country.

But this was not enough to solve Iraq's economic problems. Rebuilding costs were estimated at more than $230 billion. In desperation, Hussein asked his neighboring Arab countries to forgive Iraqi war debts. They

■ With the world against him now, Hussein tried to make over his image, at least with other Arab nations and leaders. In 1989, he met with Yasser Arafat at the Arab Summit held in Casablanca, Morocco.

refused his request after some consideration. Hussein also tried to pressure other Persian Gulf countries into controlling their oil production. Less oil meant higher demand, and higher demand meant higher prices. This would naturally mean higher profits for Iraq. But some countries regularly produced more than their quota of oil, which drove the price down. One of the main offenders was Iraq's tiny neighbor Kuwait.

Hussein was furious. He needed money badly.

Same Old Hussein

In the early months of 1990, Hussein's image makeover abruptly shattered. His political chameleon persona changed, and the world saw him in stark contrast to the moves he'd made since 1988. The old Hussein returned, full of anti-Semitic hatred and suspicion. In March 1990, Hussein executed a British journalist of Iraqi descent accused of spying. One month later, he threatened to use chemical weapons against Israel. He also lashed out at Kuwait for producing too much oil. He claimed that the country was plotting with Zionists to undermine the Arab nations. Iraqi troops began gathering on the shared border with Kuwait. By late July, more than 30,000 soldiers were camped at the edge of Kuwaiti territory.

Kuwait resisted Iraq's demands to restrict its oil production, and Hussein flew into a frenzy. He was now privately set on the path of war. But most countries—including his Arab neighbors—thought that he could be deterred. They were wrong. No country realized Hussein's true intention to invade Kuwait. Hussein needed money to survive. The oil fields of Kuwait seemed the perfect resource to rebuild Iraq's economy.

■ April Glaspie, the U.S. ambassador to Iraq during the lead-up to the First Gulf War (1991), sits for questions from the Senate Foreign Relations Committee in Washington, D.C., in March 1991. Glaspie is famous for telling Saddam Hussein that the United States did not want to get involved in problems between Iraq and Kuwait.

On July 25, a United States ambassador visited Hussein in Iraq. Hussein discussed his complaints in great detail and accused the United States of cooperating in Kuwait's "economic war" against Iraq. Ambassador April Glaspie reassured Hussein that the United States supported the Iraqi position, and that President George H. W. Bush would not declare an economic war against Iraq. She assured him that the United States had "no opinion" on the dispute with Kuwait and encouraged Iraq to solve the crisis along with other Arab states. It seemed that the

65

United States was saying a familiar message: We'll look the other way. Hussein promised the United States that he would seek a peaceful solution through official dialogue with Kuwait. But his real decision was made. The U.S. strategy of sucking up to Hussein had backfired. He thought the United States had given him the green light for war. With the impression of support from the world's only superpower, Hussein prepared to invade Kuwait.

Hussein did keep his promise to hold talks with Kuwait. On July 31, representatives from Iraq and Kuwait met in Saudi Arabia. The talks quickly disintegrated as both sides traded insults and accusations.

Crashing Kuwait

Iraqi troops blitzed into Kuwait on August 2, 1990. Kuwait's army of 16,000 didn't stand a chance against the 100,000 troops and 300 tanks that rolled into the country. Kuwait's royal family barely managed to escape its palace in a line of cars as Iraqi troops arrived at the doorstep. The invasion was over in seven hours. Hussein was overjoyed at his apparent victory.

It soon became clear, however, that the invasion of Kuwait was a major mistake for Hussein. He had sorely misjudged international support for Iraq and its case against Kuwait. Within hours he faced opposition from all corners of the globe. The United States reacted almost immediately. President Bush placed an economic embargo on Iraq and moved an aircraft carrier into the Persian Gulf. The United Nations Security Council called for an immediate withdrawal and banned all trade with Iraq. The United States froze all Iraqi and Kuwaiti money held in Western banks. On August 6, the UN signed a

■ The Iraqi army occupied Kuwait for nearly six months. Its military ran the day-to-day business of the defeated country and oversaw the population with roadblocks, checkpoints, and arrests of dissidents.

worldwide embargo on Iraq, and Turkey shut off an oil pipeline running into its country from Iraq. Hussein was suddenly in a stranglehold. Arab nations were just as shocked at the invasion. Some feared that Hussein would soon invade Saudi Arabia for its oil. They, too, demanded Hussein's retreat. He stood alone.

Against the World

Thirty countries began forming a massive military force in Saudi Arabia designed to protect the other gulf states

■ Operation Desert Shield combined nearly a million soldiers from dozens of countries in its buildup to liberating Kuwait. Here, an American soldier stands guard during early operations.

and persuade Hussein to withdraw from Kuwait. Known as Operation Desert Shield, this force contained more than 430,000 soldiers from the United States alone. The United Nations backed up this threat of force with a deadline of January 15, 1991. If Iraq did not withdraw peacefully before this deadline, the international troops were free to attack.

Hussein began his scramble for survival as the clock ticked. He found little support from Arab neighbors and even less from the international community. When the conflict began, there were more than a million foreigners working on Iraqi soil. In a desperate move, Hussein held thousands of Westerners hostage. He threatened to use them as "human shields" at important targets like power plants and military bases. He hoped that the American public would not stomach an attack on its own people. This move backfired. Public opinion was that Hussein was an evil man.

In December, Hussein released the hostages. Perhaps he hoped that the world would appreciate this act of goodwill. As January 15 approached, the United Nations offered to negotiate a plan for withdrawal. Hussein refused. To retreat from Kuwait would mean to admit a mistake and admit defeat. He could not appear to be weak. Hussein had backed into his own trap. Faced with overwhelming force, Hussein chose to stand and fight.

CHAPTER SEVEN
HUSSEIN'S SLIDE

■ The air war against Iraq struck hard at Baghdad. The skies erupted with antiaircraft fire as U.S. warplanes destroyed targets inside the capital on the morning of January 18, 1991.

On January 16, the gathered forces in the gulf unleashed a paralyzing air attack on Baghdad. Hussein appeared on television and told the world that "the mother of all battles" had begun. He pledged victory for Iraq. His answer to the air attacks was a barrage of Scud missiles that targeted cities in Israel. Hussein hoped to draw other Arab states into the war by forcing Israel to strike back. The United States had anticipated his plan and convinced Israel to hold its fire. Hussein was alone against the world. His country was hopelessly outmatched. In early February, the coalition ground troops moved in and surrounded Iraqi soldiers. The war was over less than 100 hours later. Thousands of Iraqi troops surrendered or fled. As many as 150,000 Iraqi soldiers died in the fighting.

On February 28, Hussein agreed to a UN cease-fire. He immediately declared this obvious defeat to be a shining victory for the Iraqi people and Arabs everywhere. The Americans had withdrawn, and Hussein was still standing. In his mind, they did not dare attack a great leader such as Saddam Hussein. As always, his propaganda machine ran full-force to cast him in the most positive light. Some Arab countries shared his feelings. Jordan and Egypt both saw the cease-fire as a victory for Hussein.

Meanwhile, many people in the world scratched their heads in confusion. It was clear to them that Iraq had been hopelessly overpowered. They wanted the Americans to drive deeper into Iraq and remove Hussein. But President Bush insisted that his job had been to liberate Kuwait. He encouraged the people of Iraq to overthrow Hussein themselves. Bush also feared that others in the region, such as Iran, would try to use the situation to their advantage.

The people of Iraq did try to overthrow Hussein. Kurds in the north and Shiites in the south rose up in

■ In 1991, U.S. president George H. W. Bush encouraged the Iraqi people to overthrow Hussein. No help came from the United States, and thousands of Iraqis were slaughtered. Here, Kurdish guerrillas prepare for possible attacks in the allied-occupied areas of northern Iraq.

rebellion. The result was all too familiar: Hussein's Republican Guard, an elite military force, slaughtered thousands of citizens until order was restored. By June 1991, the country was once again firmly under his control. UN sanctions, however, were erasing the last signs of Iraq's former glory.

Running Out of Gas

Iraq's economy had supported the region, and it was now sputtering. Hussein had already begun to destroy his own economy with invasions of Iran and Kuwait. The UN sanctions merely hastened the decline. Iraqi consumers couldn't afford to travel and spend, and that meant less money flowing through the Middle East. Jordan lost $1 billion per year in yearly exports when the sanctions began. By 2002, the Arab world's populations were growing twice as fast as their economies.

Arab countries watched in dismay as the slow stranglehold of UN sanctions squeezed money out of all Middle East pocketbooks. Hussein's mad designs for glory had plunged his own country into ruin and had hurt his neighbors as well. Iraq's economy had been the engine of the region. In the 1980s, Iraq had employed workers from all over the Arab world who sent money home to their families. Hussein had brought in engineers, scientists, teachers, and bankers to contribute to the glory of Iraq. Baghdad ordered imports from Lebanon, Syria, Egypt, Turkey, Saudi Arabia, and Jordan. In turn, these countries bought oil, electronics, and other imports from Iraq. Iraq was the Arab world's first modern economy. Iraq's immense wealth stabilized the Middle East when oil prices plummeted in the mid-1980s.

My Two Sons

Perhaps the true measure of Saddam Hussein is his performance as a father. Hussein raised his sons, Uday and Qusay, to view even the cruelest violence and torture as a normal event. As children they played with disarmed grenades. As boys they accompanied their father to the torture chamber while prisoners were mutilated. Hussein hoped to groom his sons in his image: a master of power and controlled violence.

This violent upbringing produced two very different men. Uday, two years older than Qusay, was loud and cocky. He drove fast cars and wore flashy clothing. His temper was legendary, and his behavior often careened out of control. When people on the street saw Uday coming, they usually ran in the other direction. Uday controlled much of Iraq's media empire. He also directed the Iraqi Olympic soccer team and was known to beat and torture the players after a poor performance.

Qusay was the quiet killer of the two. His calm confidence and willingness to kill reminded many in Iraq of Saddam Hussein himself. Qusay seemed to be in the best position to inherit Hussein's regime. Qusay controlled the elite Republican Guard and military intelligence services as well as Hussein's personal security.

Saddam Hussein's sons, Qusay and Uday

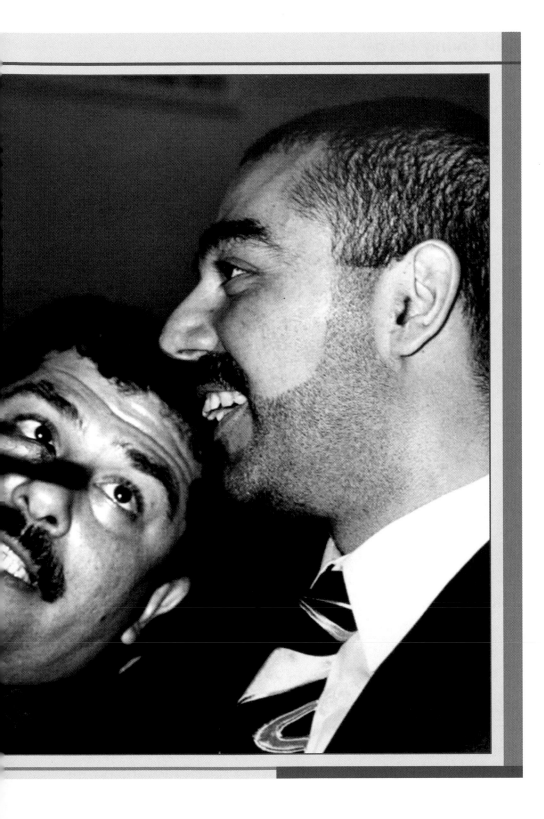

Still Living Large

The sanctions did little to change Hussein's lifestyle. His family lived the life of royalty. Sajida flew all over the world on lavish shopping sprees. Uday drank himself into wild rages and sprayed the air with bullets from one of his many machine guns. Hussein openly took mistresses into his bed. Uday was outraged at this insult to his mother and shot the man who supplied Hussein with mistresses. Hussein was outraged and jailed his oldest son, then expelled him from the country. After a short stay in Switzerland, Uday returned to Baghdad and resumed his psychopathic ways. This family was clearly above the law.

Hussein always had his eye on history and his legacy to Iraq. He did not only want to rule Iraq during his lifetime; he wanted to be remembered for thousands of years to come. He wanted to be mentioned in the same breath as Arab rulers such as Nebuchadnezzar and Saladin. As UN sanctions crippled the flow of money into Iraq, Hussein pressed on with his building projects. Walls of new buildings contained bricks with the words "Built in the era of Saddam Hussein." He began constructing the world's largest mosque as thousands of children died in hospitals without medical supplies. Within the mosque was a copy of the Koran written in Hussein's own blood, drawn from his veins over many months. Forty-three minarets rose within sight of thousands of malnourished and starving children.

Hussein's Sanctions Show

Hussein delighted in the starving and dying children in Baghdad's hospitals. They were the perfect political tool.

■ Hussein's eldest son, Uday, was supposed to succeed his father as leader of Iraq. But during the 1990s, Uday's behavior became murderous and psychotic. His father then moved his younger son, Qusay, up in the chain of command.

He invited journalists to tour the wards full of children in desperate need of medical supplies. He blamed their condition on the West and the sanctions of the United Nations. He told the Iraqi people that the sanctions were the reason for empty medical shelves.

But the truth was not so simple. The UN sanctions did not apply to humanitarian aid. Hussein was allowed to sell $1.6 billion worth of oil to purchase food and medicine for his people. Hussein refused the terms, saying that he would not let the UN tell him how to use Iraq's oil. He was too proud to back down on the world stage, and his people paid the price.

Playing the Game

Throughout the 1990s, Hussein played a continuous game of cat and mouse with the international community. This was a game he was beginning to perfect. He tested the administration of the United States in what became known as "cheat and retreat." In 1996, Hussein finally agreed to the terms of the UN sanctions. Food and medicine began to flow to his people. Then, in 1998, Hussein kicked out the UN weapons inspectors from Iraq and told them never to return. The United States and Britain responded with a four-day flurry of missile strikes, but they did little damage.

At home, he pitted his own officers against each other, always on the lookout for any threats to his power. Some holes were beginning to show in Hussein's security network. Uday was partially paralyzed in 1996 in an assassination attempt. The attackers disappeared. With his older son recovering, Hussein groomed his younger son, Qusay, to follow in his footsteps.

■ United Nations weapons inspectors arrive at a suspected weapons
site. Hussein's game of hide-and-seek frustrated the weapons inspectors. In late 1998, all of the UN weapons inspectors left Iraq under
orders from Saddam Hussein.

Never Grow Old

Hussein's newest enemy was age. Now over sixty, he fought to maintain the image of youth and command that was so important to the regime. He dyed his hair and mustache to remove the streaks of gray. Every morning began with a swim to ease the pain in his aching back. The pain was so bad that he walked with a slight limp. Television crews were not allowed to film Hussein walking more than a few steps. He could not appear weak in front of the people. Within the walls of his palaces the limp was obvious. Tailored suits hid the belly that now poked over his belt. His eyes were failing, but Hussein refused to wear reading glasses in public. His speeches were printed in huge letters with just a few lines on each page. Nonetheless, his grip on power remained firm. It appeared that he was safe from invasion as long as he stayed within his borders.

CHAPTER EIGHT
ENDGAME

The two towers of the World Trade Center smoke after being hit by jet airliners piloted by Al Qaeda's suicidal hijackers. The Bush administration has tried to link Saddam Hussein with Al Qaeda, but no proof of any connection has been found.

The entire world changed on September 11, 2001. Two commercial airplanes slammed into the towers of the World Trade Center in New York City. Minutes later a third plane crashed into the Pentagon outside

■ One segment of the huge Pentagon building smolders from a third hijacked plane on September 11, 2001. The Bush administration used the threat of further terrorism to wage war on Hussein and Iraq.

Washington, D.C. A fourth plane seemed headed for either the White House or Capitol until passengers on board attacked hijackers in the cockpit. That plane crashed into a Pennsylvania field.

The hijacked planes had been part of a coordinated terrorist attack. Soon the smoking hulks of both Trade Center towers fell to the ground. More than 3,000 people were killed. The United States began looking for those responsible even as the dust settled. One of their first suspects was Saddam Hussein.

The trail of the terrorists was soon traced to the Saudi exile Osama bin Laden, a radical Muslim. Bin Laden had worked with American intelligence agencies during the Soviet-Afghanistan war during the 1980s. After the Soviets withdrew from Afghanistan, bin Laden turned against the United States. He now operated several terrorist-training camps in Afghanistan. The son of President George H. W. Bush of the First Gulf War was now the new president of the United States. President George W. Bush declared an American "war on terror."

Saddam Hussein

مُجاهد إسلام
أُسامه بن لادن

نُورِ خُدا هے کفر کی حرکت پہ خندہ زن
پُھونکوں سے یہ چراغ بُجھایا نہ جائے گا

■ In an Al Qaeda classroom in Afghanistan, U.S. Navy SEALs (an acronym for sea, air, land) found Osama bin Laden propaganda posters tacked onto walls. Bin Laden publicly denounced Saddam Hussein as an infidel many times. It appears unlikely that the Al Qaeda financier ever dealt with Hussein's brutal regime.

Military planners immediately began to devise retaliation strikes in Afghanistan.

Hussein and bin Laden

For now it appeared that Iraq was not directly involved in the September 11 attacks on America. Hussein, however, did little to distance himself from the actions of the terrorists. He published an open letter in October that criticized America's military action in Afghanistan. He suggested that America might fall victim to further

L ife Under Hussein

Here is a glimpse at life under Saddam Hussein before his downfall. Every media outlet in Iraq bore the mark of Hussein or his sons. The government controlled news outlets. Uday Hussein monitored the media empire of radio, newspapers, and television. Every day the newspaper carried a picture of Hussein on the front page.

Interested in seeing a movie? You might have had a tough time. Forget about American movies. They were illegal. Most movies came from Egypt,

Saddam Hussein awards the Medal of Valor to his elder son, Uday.

India, and France. Government officials censored them before people could see them. Sometimes bootleg Hollywood movies were shown on YouthTV, also run by Uday. Otherwise, all there was for Iraqi citizens to see were programs about Saddam Hussein or the glories of Iraqi history.

Can't part with your cell phone? You would not have wanted to live in Iraq during the time of Saddam—they were illegal. Also, Iraqis needed government approval before sending a fax or making a photocopy. Defying this order would have gotten you in big trouble. Iraq's first Internet café opened in July 2000, but it wasn't exactly like being connected to the World Wide Web. The government censored Internet surfing, too.

terrorist attacks on its own soil. The Iraqi government proclaimed Osama bin Laden as the "Man of the Year 2001" for his devotion to Islam and his defiance of the United States. The United Nations was suspicious enough to demand access to Iraq again. It wanted to search for biological, chemical, and nuclear weapons—weapons of mass destruction. Hussein flatly refused. To date there has been no evidence found linking Saddam Hussein with Osama bin Laden's Al Qaeda organization or the September 11 attacks.

Target: Hussein

President George W. Bush soon widened his war on terror to include Iraq. He demanded that Saddam Hussein allow inspectors back into the country or face invasion. Much of the world was alarmed. Britain was the only major country to support the U.S. position on war.

On November 8, 2002, the Security Council of the United Nations passed Resolution 1441. This demanded that Iraq allow weapons inspectors back into the country and turn over all weapons of mass destruction. The resolution threatened "severe consequences" if these conditions were not met. Although the resolution did not specify any consequences, the Bush administration was hinting at war if its demands were not met. A team of UN inspectors arrived in Iraq in December and began combing the country for hidden weapons.

Once again Hussein began his scramble for survival. His cat-and-mouse games with inspectors continued. Trucks were seen driving away as inspectors arrived at suspected sites. Hussein had played this game before. He

■ Arab foreign ministers met in Cairo, Egypt, on November 10, 2002, to discuss UN Resolution 1441, adopted by the fifteen-member UN Security Council. Resolution 1441 detailed new procedures for UN weapons inspectors and tougher guidelines that Iraq must conform to.

knew that his best strategy was to draw out the conflict and gain international support. He appeared on CBS television with anchor Dan Rather in a rare interview. Looking relaxed and confident, Hussein spoke of the innocence of Iraq and the evil advance of the United States. He was clearly trying to win the hearts and minds of television viewers across the world. Few countries supported an actual war against Iraq. Hussein hoped to turn the tide against the thought of invading Iraq.

Meanwhile, President George W. Bush was determined to stop Hussein's game for the last time. The Bush administration sent more than 300,000 troops to Saudi Arabia and other stations in the Persian Gulf. British troops arrived in Kuwait. These troops awaited the order to unleash war against the defiant Hussein.

A few countries supported the American and British military buildup and the likely war. But this time around, not so many countries were willing to send troops. They backed the effort with words, equipment, and promises of money to rebuild Iraq after the war.

The Ultimatum

On March 17, 2003, President Bush gave Hussein and his sons forty-eight hours to leave Iraq or face war. Hussein remained defiant. He threatened to take the war "wherever there is sky, land, or water." Coalition forces tightened their grip around Iraq. Two hundred fifty thousand troops on all sides awaited the order to invade. The minutes ticked by, drawing closer to the deadline set by President Bush.

The War Begins

Minutes after the deadline passed, missiles lit up the sky off the coast of Iraq. They streaked fire through the blackness and headed toward a secret target: a bunker deep underground in Baghdad. President Bush soon came on television and informed the people of the United States and the world that war had begun. The United States had received a reliable tip that Hussein might be in the middle of a military meeting accompanied by both of his sons. The United States hoped to

■ One of President Saddam Hussein's palaces burns along the Tigris River in Baghdad on March 20, 2003. American missiles rained down on Baghdad during the first phase of the assault on Iraq.

decapitate the regime before the war even began by removing Hussein himself.

The smoke rising from the rubble did not produce any answers, only questions. Over the next several days the question remained: Was Hussein dead or alive? Iraqi television broadcast a tape of Hussein reading a statement denouncing the war that they said proved his survival. The man on the tape looked bloated and tired, not the trim and confident Hussein that the world had seen on television with Dan Rather only weeks earlier. U.S. intelligence services analyzed the tape and said that they believed it was indeed Hussein. But when was the tape recorded?

These questions weren't answered as coalition forces pushed into Iraq. British and American troops began a ground assault in the southern tip of the country, aiming straight toward the capital city.

The Ripple Through the Arab World

Arab countries looked on in concern as the war's impact spread throughout the region. Trade with Iraq halted when the war started. Oil prices rose sharply on the world market. Foreign investors pulled their money out of the region. The World Bank's chief economist for the region said that Jordan was at the edge of a recession. Egypt, Morocco, and Tunisia were also hit hard economically. These countries rely on tourism as a major source of revenue, but tourists were steering clear of troubled areas. Some oil-rich countries such as Iran, Yemen, and Algeria were expected to profit from higher oil prices.

■ These video frames show the sequence of Hussein's statue being toppled by the U.S. military. The taking of Baghdad was a day of celebration for most Iraqis. Following that day, the hunt for Hussein and his band of killers intensified.

The End

After a three-week fight, coalition forces entered the walls of Baghdad. The dominoes of Hussein's regime began to fall. Chemical Ali was thought to be killed in the southern town of Basra, buried under the rubble of his house after a surgical missile strike. Tribesmen captured Hussein's half-brother as he tried to flee to Syria. The head of Iraq's nuclear program, Jaffar al-Jaffar, turned himself in. Hussein's science adviser surrendered and insisted that Iraq possessed no weapons of mass destruction. As weeks passed, more members of Hussein's inner circle were captured.

Hussein's grip on power had finally crumbled. The people of Iraq stormed the city in an explosion of emotion that ranged from joy to violence. Crowds of looters stormed the presidential palace. Museums and office buildings were stripped bare. Millions of people around the world watched on television as American forces toppled a 40-foot (12 m) statue of Saddam Hussein in the center of Baghdad. The statue groaned and crashed to the ground, and a new era began in Iraq.

■ Just days before the fall of Baghdad, Saddam Hussein was shown on Iraqi television visiting homes and neighborhoods. It's not known for sure if the person in the video was Hussein. The Butcher of Baghdad was known to have many lookalikes he used for public appearances.

Alive—or Dead?

Saddam Hussein was nowhere to be found as Iraqi citizens reclaimed the streets. He was last spotted on April 8, standing atop a car and speaking to supporters in a Baghdad neighborhood as smoke from gunfights rose in the distance. The city fell the next day. When his regime finally tumbled, Saddam left behind an impressive list of titles and honors. He was secretary of the Regional Command and chairman of the Revolutionary Command Council. He was deputy secretary-general of the National Command. He was president of the republic, prime minister, and commander in chief of the Iraqi Armed Forces. But this list of titles could not change one fact. In the end, Saddam never achieved his dream of becoming a great military commander. His military conflicts all ended in a draw or a resounding defeat. Although he claimed victory to the end, Saddam Hussein led his people and his country into financial ruin. His will to survive at any cost thrust Iraq on a roller coaster ride that lasted thirty years.

Not Over Yet

The crazy ride continued for the people of Iraq as coalition forces moved into Baghdad. For weeks and months, people all over the world wondered if Saddam was alive or dead. Many people suspected that he was alive and still in Iraq. Their suspicions were soon confirmed. On July 4, an audio recording surfaced of Saddam encouraging the people of Iraq to continue the fight against their foreign invaders. He told Iraqis to "act and do not let the occupying forces settle down in your land." Many in Iraq seemed to heed his call. The transition had not been

■ A U.S. tank stands guard outside the Jordanian Embassy in Baghdad following a bomb attack on August 7, 2003. The car bomb killed seventeen people. Those responsible are still unknown but are believed to be either Hussein supporters or holy war terrorists from neighboring countries.

easy and anger ran high. Thousands of Iraqis went weeks without electricity. Looters roamed the streets.

Guerrilla fighters attacked coalition forces on a daily basis. In July 2003, three months after the official end of combat, the death toll of coalition forces surpassed that of the First Gulf War.

Striking from the Shadows

Support for Saddam ran high in the "Sunni Triangle" north of Baghdad. The Sunni Triangle is home to many

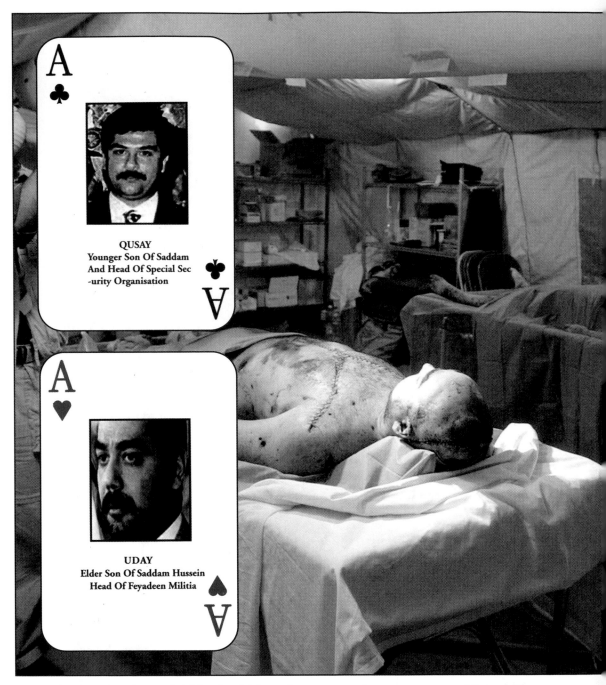

■ On April 11, 2003, the U.S. military issued a most wanted list of fifty-five Iraqis in the form of a deck of cards. Qusay and Uday Hussein were numbers two and three on that list. The Hussein brothers died in a gun battle on July 22, 2003, against the U.S. military.

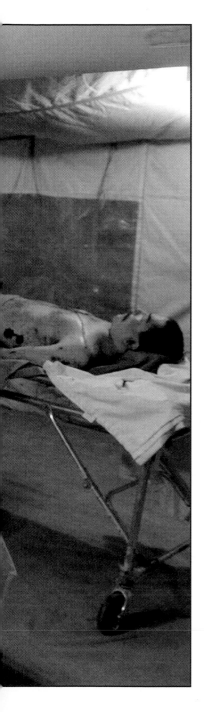

of Iraq's Sunni Muslims. Sunni Muslims held great power under Hussein's rule. Despite this power, Sunnis comprise only 20 percent of Iraq's population. Plans for Iraq's new government promised more power to the Shiite Muslim majority. Hussein had been the Sunnis' only hope to retain the upper hand. It was clear that Saddam and his sons were running with the hope that a guerrilla war would eventually restore their hold on power. But how long could they hide?

On the morning of July 22, coalition forces caught up with Uday and Qusay. The brothers had been hiding out in a wealthy neighborhood in Mosul. The owner of the house decided to hand over the brothers in exchange for the reward money of $30 million. The brothers finally perished in a furious gunfight that raged for six hours. On July 29, Saddam mourned their passing in a new audiotape, but he remained defiant: "Even if Saddam Hussein has one hundred children other than Uday and Qusay, Saddam Hussein would offer them the same way. Thank God for what He destined for us and honored us with their martyrdom for His sake."

addam ussein

The Master of Survival

The net was closing in on Saddam. Coalition forces captured six of his bodyguards. Soldiers swooped in predawn raids on Tikrit farms. But Saddam remained elusive. The attacks on troops continued. Iraq remained divided between the promise of a new future and the shadow of its old leader. As the country picks up the pieces and begins a new era, many citizens are probably watching the shadows. They expect to see Saddam Hussein lurking there, planning his next chance at greatness.

1937 Saddam Hussein born on April 28 in
Tikrit, Iraq.

1955 Hussein graduates from primary school and
moves to Baghdad.

1957 Joins the Arab Baath Socialist Party.

1959 Baath Party assassins, including Hussein, attempt
to murder the Iraqi prime minister. The
attempt fails and Hussein flees to Syria.

1963 Hussein returns to Iraq after government is
overthrown.

1964 Hussein's first son, Uday, is born on June 18.
Hussein is arrested and imprisoned by the Iraqi
government for undermining the regime.

1966 Hussein escapes from prison.

1968 In July, Hussein participates in the Baath Party
coup that overthrows the Iraqi government.

1969 On November 9, Hussein is elected vice chairman
of the Revolutionary Command Council.

1979 On July 16, Hussein is elected as president of Iraq
and chairman of the Revolutionary Command
Council. Six days later Hussein stages the his-
toric purge of the Command Council.

1980 Hussein orders attack of Iranian air bases on
September 22. This attack begins the Iran-
Iraq War.

1988 A cease-fire with Iran is finally instituted on
August 8.

1990 Iraq invades and seizes Kuwait on August 2.

1991 The United States and coalition forces begin bombing Iraq on January 16 after Hussein refuses to leave Kuwait.

The First Persian Gulf War ends on February 28 with Hussein's agreement to a UN cease-fire.

1993 Hussein breaks the peace terms from the end of the Persian Gulf War.

1998 Hussein fails to comply with UN weapons inspectors. This results in a four-day bombing raid by the United States in October.

U.N. inspectors leave Iraq in December.

2001 On September 11, the World Trade Center towers in New York City and the Pentagon in Washington, D.C., are attacked. This raises suspicions of Hussein and links to terror organizations, but Hussein is never connected with the attacks.

2002 Hussein allows return of UN weapons inspectors under growing international pressure.

2003 On March 17, President George W. Bush gives Hussein an ultimatum: either leave Iraq within 48 hours or be attacked. On March 19, United States and British forces invade Iraq.

Baghdad falls on April 9.

Saddam's sons, Uday and Qusay, are killed in a gunfight with coalition forces on July 22.

Saddam releases an audiotape on July 24, praising his sons as martyrs.

The hunt continues for Saddam.

anti-Semitism Relating to or characterized by a racist hating of Jews.

assassin One who murders by surprise attack, especially one who carries out a plot to kill a prominent person.

ayatollah A high-ranking Shiite religious authority in matters of religious law and interpretation.

clan A group of people related by blood or marriage.

coalition An alliance, especially a temporary one, of people, factions, parties, or nations.

deter To prevent or discourage from action.

embargo A prohibition by a government on some or all trade with a foreign nation.

exile The enforced removal from one's native country.

Kurds A pastoral and agricultural people inhabiting the transnational region of Kurdistan in southwest Asia, which is within the boundaries of Iraq, Iran, Turkey, Syria, and Armenia.

nationalism Devotion to the interests or culture of one's nation; the desire for national independence in a country under foreign domination.

propaganda Information that is spread for the purpose of promoting some cause or system of beliefs.

purge To rid (a nation or political party, for example) of something considered undesirable.

regime A government or administration in power.

rural Of or relating to people who live in the country.

sanction A usually economic measure taken against a country that has violated a moral principle or international law.

Shiite A member of the branch of Islam that regards Ali as the legitimate successor to Muhammad. Shiites do not acknowledge Sunnis as any part of the Muslim law.

Sunni A member of the branch of Islam that accepts the first four caliphs as rightful successors to Muhammad rather than Ali.

Zionism A Jewish movement that sought to reestablish a Jewish homeland in Palestine. Modern Zionism is concerned with the support and development of the state of Israel.

FOR MORE INFORMATION ★ ★ ★

RESOURCES

Organizations

Americans for Middle East Understanding
475 Riverside Drive, Room 245
New York, NY 10115-0245
(212) 870-2053
Web site: http://www.ameu.org

Amnesty International
322 Eighth Avenue
New York, NY 10001
(212) 807-8400
Web site: http://www.amnestyusa.org

Centre for Arab Unity Studies
Lyon Street—Sadat Tower Building
P.O. Box Hamra Beirut 1103 2090
Beirut, Lebanon
Tel: +961-1-801587 / 801582 / 869164
Web site: http://www.caus.org.lb

Council on American-Islamic Relations (CAIR)
453 New Jersey Avenue SE
Washington, DC 20003
(202) 488-8787
Web site: http://www.cair-net.org

Human Rights Watch (HRW)
350 Fifth Avenue, 34th Floor
New York, NY 10118-3299
(212) 290-4700
Web site: http://www.hrw.org

Iraqi American Council
1220 L Street NW, Suite 100-262
Washington DC 20005-4018
(800) 416-8684
Web site: http://www.iraqiamericans.com

Middle East Studies Association of North America
c/o The University of Arizona
1219 North Santa Rita Avenue
Tucson, AZ 85721
(520) 621-5850
e-mail: mesana@u.arizona.edu
Web site: http://w3fp.arizona.edu/mesassoc

United States Department of State
2201 C Street NW
Washington, DC 20520
(202) 647-4000
Web site: http://www.state.gov

Veterans of Foreign Wars of the United States
National Headquarters
406 West 34th Street
Kansas City, MO 64111
(816) 756-3390
e-mail: info@vfw.org
Web site: http://www.vfw.org

Wisconsin Project on Nuclear Arms Control
1701 K Street NW, Suite 805
Washington, DC 20006
(202) 223-8299
Web site: http://www.iraqwatch.org

Web Sites

Due to the changing nature of Internet links, the Rosen Publishing Group, Inc., has developed an online list of Web sites related to the subject of this book. This site is updated regularly. Please use this link to access the list:

http://www.rosenlinks.com/mel/shus

★ ★ ★ FOR FURTHER READING

Anderson, Dale. *Saddam Hussein.* New York: Lerner Publishing Company, 2003.

Bard, Mitchell, Ph.D. *The Complete Idiot's Guide to Middle East Conflict.* Indianapolis: Alpha Books, 1999.

Claypool, Jane. *Saddam Hussein.* Vero Beach, FL: Rourke Publications, 1993.

Deegan, Paul, and Rosemary Wallner, ed. *Saddam Hussein.* Edina, MN: Abdo & Daughters, 1991.

Mance, Angelia L. *Iraq.* Philadelphia: Chelsea House Publishing, 2002.

Shields, Charles J. *Saddam Hussein.* Philadelphia: Chelsea House Publishing, 2002.

Stefoff, Rebecca. *Saddam Hussein: Absolute Ruler of Iraq.* Brookfield, MA: Millbrook Press, 1995.

Tripp, Charles. *A History of Iraq.* New York: Cambridge University Press, 2000.

BIBLIOGRAPHY ★ ★ ★

Bard, Mitchell, Ph.D. *The Complete Idiot's Guide to Middle East Conflict.* Indianapolis: Alpha Books, 1999.

Bowden, Mark. "Tales of the Tyrant." *Atlantic Monthly*, May 2002, Vol. 289, Issue 5, p. 35.

Coughlin, Con. *Hussein: King of Terror.* New York: HarperCollins, 2002.

Dickey, Christopher, et al. "How Hussein Happened." *Newsweek*, September 23, 2002, Vol. 140, Issue 13, p. 34.

Dickey, Christopher, Rod Norland, and John Barry. "Palace Intrigue." *Newsweek* (Atlantic Edition), October 14, 2002, Vol. 140, Issue 16, p. 14.

Glain, Stephen. "Hussein the Builder." *Newsweek* (Atlantic Edition), March 11, 2002, Vol. 139, Issue 10, p. 30.

Karsh, Efraim, and Inari Rautsi. *Saddam Hussein: A Political Biography.* New York: The Free Press, 1991.

Munthe, Turi, ed. *The Saddam Hussein Reader: Selections from Leading Writers on Iraq.* New York: Thunder's Mouth Press, 2002.

"Hussein's Charm Offensive." *The Economist*, October 12, 2002, Vol. 365, Issue 8294, p. 57.

Stefoff, Rebecca. *Saddam Hussein: Absolute Ruler of Iraq.* Brookfield, MA: Millbrook Press, 1995.

Thomas, Evan, et al. "Hussein's Sons." *Newsweek* (Atlantic Edition), October 21, 2002, Vol. 140, Issue 17, p. 48.

"World Bank: War Rocks Mideast Economies, Jordan in Particular." Middle East North Africa Financial Network, April 12, 2003. Retrieved April 2003 (http://www.menafn.com/qn_print.asp?StoryID=17601&subl=true).

Yahia, Latif, and Karl Wendl. *I Was Hussein's Son*. New York: Arcade Publishing, 1997.

Yourish, Karen. "Iraq's Troubled Terrain." *Newsweek*, September 23, 2002, Vol. 140, Issue 13, p. 38.

About the Author

Brian Wingate graduated from the University of North Carolina at Chapel Hill with a degree in Sociocultural Anthropology. His interest in the world's cultures led him around the globe, including journeys in Turkey, Iran, and Morocco. Brian now lives in the United States with his family.

Photo Credits

Front cover map courtesy of the Library of Congress; front cover image, pp. 40, 74–75, 81, 82–83, 84, 96–97 © Reuters New Media Inc./Corbis; flags on back cover and pp. 1, 3, 16, 27, 39, 48, 58, 70, 81, 96 (playing cards), 98, 100, 102, 104, 106, 107, 109 © Nelson Sá; p. 1 © Alain Nogues/Corbis; pp. 3 (chapter 1 box), 6, 8–9, 42–43 © Perry-Castañedia Library Map Collection/The University of Texas at Austin; pp. 3 (chapter 2, 4, 7, 8 boxes), 4, 10–11, 14, 16, 22, 24–25, 39, 45, 79, 90–91, 92–93 © AP/Wide World Photos; pp. 3 (chapter 3 box), 27, 30–31, 36, 48, 50, 52 © Hulton Archive/Getty Images; pp. 3 (chapter 5 box), 56–57 © Francoise de Mulder/Corbis; pp. 3 (chapter 6 box), 33, 58 © Sygma/Corbis; p. 18 © Hulton-Deutsch Collection/Corbis; pp. 28–29 © Bettmann/Corbis; pp. 34–35 © Vittoriano Rastelli/Corbis; p. 60 © Jacques Langevin/Corbis; pp. 62–63 © Maher Attar/Corbis; pp. 64–65 © Marcy Nighswander/AP/Wide World Photos; pp. 66–67 © Salah Masrawi/AP/Wide World Photos; pp. 68, 77, 85, 86–87 © Corbis; p. 70 © Dominique Mollard/AP/Wide World Photos; pp. 72–73 © Burhan Ozbilici/AP/Wide World Photos; pp. 88–89 © Ali Heider/AP/Wide World Photos; pp. 94–95 © Wally Sanatana/AP/Wide World Photos.

Designer: Nelson Sá; **Editor:** Mark Beyer;
Photo Researcher: Nelson Sá